Earth, Mercy

Earth, Mercy

poems

Mary Rose O'Reilley

Louisiana State University Press   *Baton Rouge*

Published with the assistance of the Sea Cliff Fund

Published by Louisiana State University Press
Copyright © 2013 by Mary Rose O'Reilley
Manufactured in the United States of America
LSU Press Paperback Original

DESIGNER: Mandy McDonald Scallan
TYPEFACES: Whitman and Gotham

Library of Congress Cataloging-in-Publication Data

O'Reilley, Mary Rose.
  Earth, mercy : poems / Mary Rose O'Reilley.
    p. cm.
  "LSU Press Paperback Original."
  ISBN 978-0-8071-4950-8 (pbk. : alk. paper) — ISBN 978-0-
8071-4951-5 (pdf) — ISBN 978-0-8071-4952-2 (epub) — ISBN
978-0-8071-4953-9 (mobi)
  I. Title.
  PS3615.R456E27 2012
  811'.6—dc23

                                         2012011757

The paper in this book meets the guidelines for permanence
and durability of the Committee on Production Guidelines for
Book Longevity of the Council on Library Resources. ∞

For Elijah and Willa O'Reilley

Contents

Acknowledgments

The land—as one turns compost under the scotch pines—yields its own kind of poems: knots of gristle and bone kicked out of an owl's nest; potsherds, ocher-patterned; the shamanic runes on river rock. The house, a century old, offers its buffalo nickels, a carpenter's penciled notes behind the wallpaper. Civilization, ephemeral as the house, gives up the fragments it has shored. Burned scraps descend with lines of music, grocery lists, the legends of Odin and his raven, anonymous medieval Marian lyrics: *as dew in Aprille that falleth on grass. . . .* A poet doesn't need to travel far on the prairie. I would like to acknowledge these influences and presences.

Two fine poets, Renée Ashley and Todd Davis, offered suggestions on early drafts of *Earth, Mercy.* "Eve's Dog" is lovingly dedicated to Renée. I would give her a better dog if I had one. Todd will know that "When Jesus Was Dying" could be written for no one but him. Thank you.

"Lindens" is for Peter Crysdale.

"The Plain Speech" is for my companion and musical partner of some thirty years, Robin Fox, who grew up in a family that used what Quakers call the Plain Speech and rarely deviates from it.

May I thank, as well, the editorial staff at LSU Press, in particular their external reviewer, who offered fierce, lengthy, and perceptive counsel, not once but twice. I am humbled by attention and generosity far surpassing the value of this work.

I am grateful to the editors of the following publications, where the poems in this book, often in different form, first appeared: *Literary Review, Orion, Ploughshares, Poetry,* and *Solo Café.* "The Third Winter" was published in *Making Poems: Forty Poems with Commentary by the Poets* (New York: State University of New York Press, 2012), edited by Todd Davis and Erin Murphy.

Earth, Mercy

Genesis

They had already fallen
into that rhythm
of loving the world;

morning and evening,
the days
stepped out

with something like footfalls,
morning and evening for eons
without a microbe or rat.

Yet there must have been
such suspension,
such breath

in that humid and green
arrival. Sometimes
a kind of prayer

takes any animal
into this warm rain,
breast of being

that loves flesh
and hopes
the new beast will come.

Eve's Dog

I used to look at her, so gold.
Not, maybe, *shallow,* as you'd think,

knowing the end of the story.
I'd nuzzle the Cloud's hand

wanting to browse the booty
myself—better at loyalty

worse at keeping the rules.
Sometimes I look at her, so gold.

She went out of the garden
snapping her ineffectual teeth

at the government,
refusing, like me, his down-stay.

I went along.

A Week without God, North Coast

NIGHT

At the end of God's word is God's silence.
Burned smell on the wind.
One of the old Fathers, at this impasse
counseled his novice to break into flame;

this option eludes me as yet
like the chokecherry's performance
all down its branch.

I have nothing inside to convert to blossom
or fire. I sit on the edge of a long drop,
as the Irish monastics patrolled their sliver
of ground, watching for God's plane.

MORNING

Each night, I go under the cliff
of your shoulder, a washed bone, stripped
and refined past the point where I think
I have nothing to lose.

Then, Morning, Bright Morning Star!
up with the north, jaywalking over the road;
O Morning, pinwheeling down,
to get me again for the day,
where I have clothes to put on,
pink thong sandals,
and something to do in the world
they give me and take away.

SPARROW HAWK

Maybe too late.

I wasted so many hours laid out with my sitter,
watching the soaps, thinking time and death
could be pulled like a plug at lunchtime.

Five days we've lived on this shore
and I get old: a girl descends rock face
a woman can't make it back,
soft moss under the slick patella eroded
gray hair tangled among the roots
of wild parsnip.

Wind up in the night, long combers
shake the foundation of our house.
High in their nest, sparrow hawks scream.
A dog careens into the bed
wanting to go outside, wanting breakfast
all that dogs want, all anyone wants: someone
to scratch the tick bite on the belly
to smell time.

I want to walk on the shore
and feel something infinite pull on my braids.
But there will be time for that after breakfast
the dog says.

ROADRUNNERS

Then God can wait.
I've waited enough for him, as a child sits

in front of the morning cartoons
lulled into despair for a world
run by Felix the Cat, rabbits,
roadrunners smashing furniture,
flattening innocent critters,
tracks of a pick-up across each resilient back;

green, two-dimensional grownups
pointing with sticks at a storm system.

I've held God's hand as a child leads
her drunken father home to the tufts
of his own sofa, turns on the test pattern,
tiptoes away.

ANNUNCIATION

I want to hold still and make nothing happen:
surely the Virgin said this, busy and dumb
as the spindle that swings from her hand.

"Listen," the angel tells her, "spin
to the motion of his will. Endure the brooding
of men who want sons for themselves."

Day after day the lake struggles against the bowl
of its life, a child hating the cradle.

Just before dawn we smell bread.
Across the bay, men and women
drive their trucks over Wolf Ridge
get into their hairnets and set out the new loaves.

I want to stand in plain space, my eyes
window shades for the moment in someone's doll
geared to spring open on strange worlds.
I want thoughts new as minnows.

Suppose she'd refused his hot morning tea?
It's not that he bothered to know what inwardness
a girl offers, standing there in the light
with her nervous grin.
What if she'd laughed at him?

Woodsman

He calls the green girls to his tent,
spirits of red pine, cedar
their hair in needles and knots.

In his dream, tree after tree
he lies with them. Ounce after
ounce, his body moves

into the woods. Celery-smelling
children, pale as new leaf,
ring him round

stare into wakening eyes.

Next to Nothing

He didn't put money into the place
thinking he'd not be there long:
considered always the salt
buddha of his life.

He never mended the frayed
edge of that shade,
planted no flowering bush.
He knew the names of things
that happened to grow.

I watched him mend
the flesh of a cottontail
torn by a dog
*though we're not short
of rabbits* he'd say,
setting it home in the garden
where nothing that came up
was meant to stay.

Lullaby of the Virgin Mary

The bread will not rise.
The infant cries.

There is a reason.
I don't know the reason.

Perhaps I did not sing
long enough to the gluten

maybe because his father
is over the water.

Go to bed, my mother said
with the child on your skin

to bring the milk in.
I am afraid

those who lie
down will not rise.

If I close my eyes
my heavy body

may steal his breath.
Already his flesh is shedding

the fur of birth.
Death comes down the hill

like a schoolbus
shifting gears.

He is leaving his animal
body *where his mother was*

as dew in Aprille
that falleth on grasse.

Ponies

Into the crèche of his father's arms,
eyeing the world's Monet.

He knows nothing
of how the man
led her along the bridge
of his love, word after word,
thirty hours. All of them here
for the first time. He knows nothing
about her constancy,
offering over and over
the gold nipple of this world.

On the threshold, jasmine's planted.
House cats take over the hollows
under the wedding quilt.

White and brown ponies
gaze over the fence
into the kitchen window.

When Jesus Was Dying

He was always singing about the world;
if there was more, he didn't count on it.

He went into the woods in shirtsleeves,
loved the smell of his rifle, its bright oil.

When Jesus was dying, he heard the clank
of dogs' tags against the dish

as they rushed their kibble. He stood in the kitchen
making the morning tea, weight of the mug

ghosted with honey glaze. Pent up in a dream
he recalled the tilt of a woman's spine

as she lay in a mattress ad. Sleep. Satiety.
In the green tongue of a leaf, its ripe strawberry.

Abandoned Farm

In the northwest corner of Dakota, I saw a room
someone had left, a plush sofa returning its button-
eyed stare to the glance she gave it over her shoulder,
the dog, too, turning. In the next room, the mattress
with mattress stories one after another tumbling
out of each spring, the window she opened first thing,
its vista of mile after mile, and the windmill hauling
its load.
    I saw that, and nothing alive—

green oil-figured linoleum laid on counters,
nails of bad craft, the ripped blackening edge
that scared her more than the bed and the sound
of the windmill winning its will from the aquifer
night after night, the whack of her blade on the block.
There are houses with too many knives sometimes she said

but when June ferned its way in she'd relent, take on its
restraint, heave again on the stained sheets her burden
of child, herself a torn girl again, combing her hair
through fingers bruised by corn shocks, sweet juice
in the cuts of her life.

              She began to think of the border
and mustangs without brand. At night they'd bend
over the bed and nuzzle. One ride was enough.
She had sufficient magic to cling to a mane and fare
over the windowsill. I see where the curtain fell
and nobody mended the tear, I see where bare feet
marked like fossils her pass in the rain.

When he uncovers fiddleheads by the spring,
why does he always think of that first sight

of her thigh in the peach-colored dress, of his hand's
searching moss with its red-gold stamens, the spring
in that arid landscape like something from Canaan
under his tongue? Even in old age he'd ponder the moment,
lying under the moon forgiving himself, her, the world
that bred their conundrum, washed in that rain.

The Plain Speech

After twenty years the love we make
we braid into the hair of the day.
Sometimes I watch each stitch in the quilt

white hairs pecking the days out,
sometimes I cry and stop you
to talk about death. Still you start

telling your beads
into my hand. *That day*
next to the slough you say

We napped in the car. Buffalo cows
stepped out of the rocks, stopped the calves
in a half-circle behind us. We could not move

or turn. They loomed at us out of the mirrors.
You wrap me in this story, a man coming home
coat full of red cyclamen. Clay strung to the roots.

After some struggle to find the true north of their lives
great and small wings return. White-throated sparrow
slow beat of cranes crossing Dakota. Orioles take

fruit we've left on a human plate. Like a farmer
suppressing his muscles for church, behind you
the uncurtained window, beside you the iron bed

you stand in your black pants, shirtsleeves,
a patch of wrinkles smelling of damp and the iron.
You call to me in the plain speech we use at home.

    Answer me *earth, mercy.*
    Answer me *rain.*

The Bridal Shower

Fresh out of Bible College,
her own white wedding
and the mission honeymoon,
she has little to say
about the unflattering dress,
her funny old title—
Matron of Honor—
and the bouquet, or the car
speeding into the circle
she'll enter a minute from now
out of control.

For hours
the three-months' husband
tries her cell; the in-laws,
the hostess, and all hands
are taking apart the centerpiece
they will lay at the intersection
later today.

The hostess is telling the cops
they drank nothing but lemonade,
wishing she hadn't held the party
up at the door for that long joke
about lingerie. How the Matron of Honor
blushed, just married
(as they keep saying)
three months.

He drives around, getting frantic.
She is on life support.
Already, someone has run up
Jesus and told them

it's meant to be.
They keep her heart going,
organ team on the tarmac.

Eyes rolling, he tries to answer
the questions, here, now,
in the sight of these witnesses
marrying, starry and spending
too much, smashing cake
on each other's faces—

How she laughed and stopped
at the door—and her heart,
it keeps beating. Somebody
wakens and wants it,
such an untested instrument,
having so little say.

Improving the Neighborhood

Red houses, white houses, drawing our curtains
against the spectacle of each other
washing dishes and trimming the dog's nails.
Now and then we exchange news. Life's
gotten harder, easier, nobody this week
has tied a noose in the master bedroom
or watched his bed flame on the lawn.
Nobody in a black auto pulled up
to take someone away.

Outside my window, mourning doves,
in their ritual, nod and bow.
I kneel in the kitchen
peeling back layer after layer
of a housewife's life,
down to the plaster and lath
of whatever she knew:
only marriage is safe enough
to contain the immense desire
with which we enter the world.
When I take up the carpets
there's blood in the cracks of the floor.

That clothesline has always stood
between two crosses; back and forth
for a hundred years
someone has pegged out the tale.
I want to see her serene and disciplined;
nobody is. We all wake often,
ice pick to the heart, with our daily list.
We envy the nodding doves.

The house keeps crying about its own boards:
think of my story, atoms, forests, oceans
sweeping the sand you gaze through
onto the street. How can you pass
over anyone's lintel
without kissing the floor,
thanking each thing that positioned its body
to make you a stair . . . her face at the window
her lamp guttering there?

That Last Time

Not even a decrescendo, much less an ovation:
people die with the TV on, nurse changing channels,
the popular shaman-psychologist set to divulge
meaning after the next commercial.
                                              I look
over my shoulder: *why was it all such a fever?*—
wanting to lie down on grass next to the boathouse,
fishing for sunnies, the dog beside me
smelling lightly of things he's rolled in—
but the nurse in green scrubs, yellow cord at the waist,
picks up the remote and, *nothing.*
                                    Think: the release
bodies offer. Home from work, feeling through silk
office blouses distended veins over the milk ducts,
symbiosis of mother and child, resting at last
cosmic as Buddha, as if we just came here to feed.
What did God know of breaking the body? Something
alive in the cells of his human brain told him to eat.

Or the dip of red bobbers, the pull of a fish, algae
splitting its millions of hairs in the lake, sun,
my skin hot: I sleep with the line loose
in my hand.
              That last time, I didn't know it was over.
Weaning is slow work; one day, without tears, the child's steps
bend away but you don't notice. You think there will be
another smell of her damp sparse hairline, another day.
Another child, maybe. Even last night, in a dream,
I thought I was bleeding again.

Even last night on the Greyhound crossing Wisconsin
I took in light from the barn, line of our hill
love's body: how you climb into bed and file
your long frame next to mine.
                                    What you imagine
is all that is left in the world. What I myself
have forgotten or not known: landscapes you paint
in a mind I can't enter. Before I knew you
there were cloakrooms, galoshes, pencil sharpeners,
irregular verbs. Still we were moving toward sleep
in each other's arms, thinking we wanted some other thing,
maybe a cocker spaniel. Not marriage, close as one breast
bone can get to a spine, what we cannot remember
and, just as we slide into sleep, what we will not say.

The Third Winter

Their implacable names:
Classen, Boelke and Fricke . . .

The girl from the next place
brings over a line of dried fish,

knowing the child died.
Every day, the wife sits

mostly in silence,
letting the windows

hold her in.
No one under these shingles

theorizes. Sometimes a poem
in the newspaper brought from town

tells them how sad they are
or gives them a look at the hay rick,

frost on the sill. She tacks it up
in the milkhouse to tell them

someone has seen their lives.
The house, she thinks,

is a body, heart on the second floor,
stomach just above frost line.

In the dugout that first winter
he entered her over and over,

thinking of rooms he would build
over the new bed,

thinking the house would have arms.

Stories of Water

No trees here: sky and snow mist rising
out of the furrows. She can't stand it.
It isn't her place. She wants red oak, pine,
vases of elm, sycamores wounded
for hundreds of years. The round gable,
its lookout on plain space, scares her. He turns
from her stories of water and claims the flat hill
he craves, high prairie threshing barn, granary
falling to ruin—They drive in, grasp the intent:
the eyes of the farm rise to meet hers, a dog's
down to the wire. It reaches back in its skin
for the price of their slow ascent, their risk
of annihilation again. The barn thinks of its Bess
and Clover, its stanchions reaching for life.

You Ask Me to Speak

We lay on the slant door of the storm
cellar just as the wind rose. Above you
cottonwood leaves began shaking.
You pulled at my dress and called me
your plate of light.
              We should have taken
shelter. White deer flee through the love
where year after year we harvest
each other, fields green with our blood.
There is no more to hope for, I tell you,
no more to feel. You interrupt deer
after deer the animals of my mind.
If I speak you will leave, looking
as if a tree told you the score, or the dog
or a crow or your own soul.

Nothing Special

In the end we left quickly, sheets
in the dryer, milk record tacked
over stalls. I can still say the name
of each cow in the order
she walked to the truck.
Neither of us took a look
over our shoulder: that option
comes back in dreams
like the heft in my hand of odd things,
nothing special, nothing the auctioneers
called *collectible*. Maybe a hammer
hung by its claw over the cream separator.
Something my dad handled.
Something I wish I had.

Warblers

Always two-by-two in the aspen
singing the *chip chip*
of good partnership.

Needing to let the other one
know his job
and her expectations for lunch.

This is no tree to be
by yourself in.

A few thoughts, big
as the New York Library,
work for them

while we reason and choose, try
out recipes. They do not envy
another one's yellow feathers,
try for a bigger nest.

Things happen as they do everywhere:
somebody hits a windshield
and doesn't get home.

I'd be lost without you
each one sings and means it.

Lindens

We left by way of the parking garage
white paint on white paint
on cream. Next to the glass
where the attendant takes money,
an orange splash. We pass a hole
where men descend into the floor:
each man grasps a pole,
steps on the lift, descends,
grim-looking always,
maybe a wrench in hand.

You in your tailored coat
with its narrow lapels, homburg precisely placed.
Winter twilight, lamps coming on,
that fox-colored lock of hair
falls over your forehead.
On the nap of your hat, snowflakes
stand out a moment, become water.

Yet—I say—*it will be cold.*

If I go back for the wool cloche
I see in my mind's hotel closet,
somehow I will lose you:
both of us frail, decorous,
trying to stay with each other,
not rousing suspicion.
Your arm under my hand,
twenty-eight bones, each cell
storing flake by flake
its crystal of snow.
If I look over my shoulder
the tracks will scare me,
ephemeral as a squirrel's.

Despite the mix of despair
and resolve both of us feel,
our strength of purpose
suspending the town
on a thread of calm,
we stop to take in that wall
white paint on white
which has not been built yet

ganzfeld

and the gray workers riding their wheel
to the underworld
where it's all deals with the gods.

Ahead, the fretwork of our bridge
and on the path we will take
a line of lindens seeded with light.

Old Lovers' Aubade

You sit up in bed
to hear the slap of the day
getting out with a gust
as we must also,
our bodies tied up
to complete each other in love.

Later, you'll say I slept.
You'll say you watched
over my sleep
like its creator
with something maternal
in your contemplation.

Trees hold out their green coins.
The elm is dying.
Last year you warned me,
watching its signs,
said little: what's to say
about flurries of seed
in an old yard?

You watch me sleep
as I watched the children.
We're both
in our devious ways
getting ready to go.
With the slyness
of wives and husbands
calling the lawyer
we visit God.

Thaw

Snow that fell clumsily into March
drips over the gutters today;
drifts quilting the garden
give up.

We come from the rooms,
revenants,
pulling the pink sponge curlers
out of our hair,
wash windows with vinegar,
call the cousins.

Even the dead
tap from the ground,
wanting to taste just
salad. An owl in the pines
knocks snow out of her nest,
kicks out her trash
of small bones.

Confession

Last night, I ate a soup bowl of ice cream
with butterscotch sauce. My basement
is full of trash I paid too much for.

I did not love my mother
and though I loved my father
I did not please him.

I take naps. For fourteen years
I couldn't forgive my ex-husband,
only hardened my heart.

My drawers are a mess.
I own too many shoes.
I don't give much money away.

There are light bulbs I ought to replace.
I don't understand foreign policy.
I've let my languages slide.

I throw out the mending.
Sometimes I pretend
to care, to listen, to be working.

I read stupid mystery stories,
criticize. Also the dog
does not obey me.

Absolution

What's the matter with you?
I ask myself in my mother's voice
as if I would tell her.

There must be something wrong,
I continue,
you can't and you won't and you don't—

If I talked to the dog that way
she'd say *damn right*
and I don't reason about it.

Turn your back.
Stretch out four legs to the sky
and sleep.

What's wrong with a grovel
for petting and treats?
All that you do—the dog says—

is perfect.

Key Lime Pie

Commas of lime in sugar and milk,
suspension, mild on the tongue
as memory of being filled,
or if you never were full before,
now is the moment—
be born again,
trailing, for all I care,
Augustine, Ambrose, all of those guys—

Aquinas, sit here, eat this pie.
Each one's longing to feel
a belly round with surfeit,
figuring out at last
one of the *why's* we came for:
key lime pie.

Tumble with me, Augustine,
out of the pear tree of self-hate.
Here is a Buddha-pie your African grin
can barely take in. Here is a radical
home-coming pie. Aquinas,
it runs down your chin.
You will never again
have to be clever or even good.

Taste the green skin of *logos*
wanting to kiss your tongue.
You are undone, like a child
gone feral to smell grass,
murmuring *here it is,*
all I have longed for
at last, at last.

Burning the House

Looking over my shoulder
I see the house I built
on fire

the roof line gaudy with flame,
each window a proof
for fire's geometry.

Well, I was leaving anyway,
dog at my heel. Some crocodile
has your watch

in his mouth.
The knock on the door
will not be a dark stranger

coming to bear you away
on a palfrey
somewhere without sidewalks.

It's the Jehovah's Witnesses,
kids begging you to buy candy
to keep them out of the gangs.

Don't get nailed down.
Whistle the dog of your life
and go on.

Trying to Get Home

The map, wrinkled and pleated,
lies under the passenger seat

with ketchup bottles and soda cans.
We keep cars so long in this family

it seems like the map of another life.
Lost, strayed? He wants it

wants the familiar pink lacquered
point of her finger tracing its lines

telling him where to turn.
The map, she says, as she always says,

will not get us there. Bridges are out
traffic rerouted, cars spinning their wheels

on the edge. She licks her thumb,
works at a stain on the blue highway

that won't take them home.
He turns on the high lights

which only refract eyes
to the left and right

glittering,
a pair of them hers.

The Architect

She pushes aside the curtain.
Out there the river

over the river the bridge
spun out of a man's mind

thinking about his wife
foreknowing it all:

jumpers and blood, eagles.
This will not fall

he tells her, finding no other words
to assuage her fear.

Deep in his sisters' garden
their fairy walls—fragile

laughable really—
entrap him at each turn

in the marriage bed.
He wakes shaking

off delicate cities,
finds her upon the stair.

Earthquake

The earthquake was always here.
Now it turns over in bed.
The facade of our house

falls into the street
our rooms on view.
We paid too much

for those curtains
the vacuum cleaner from Sears,
its attached gadgets.

I just want to ask
did the dog get out?
There were no children

long ago they escaped
these rooms. Looting
begins. My fur coat

goes by. Pearl
survivors of some oyster
wreck. I remember the day

I bought that sofa.
I remember desire.
I liked the feeling

of being a face
at that window
wanting it all.

The Workbench

The men who came here after you left
like the tools: your Craftsman wrenches,
planes trimmed with bronze,
the t-square, the billie, the adze.

I could bring you the thing
you cried for on top of the ladder
and when, from behind the fence,
you pronounced the word *scythe,*
I would find it.

Blood

The dead of this house
watch me pick up the newspaper,

they plunge their hands
into the dishwater

of every day;
they come to lie

beside the body
of anyone's love

as I would. They lick
the blood of a small wound,

stare
out of the mirror

at a woman
just parting her hair.

Plum

Quince flames on the wall,
I look for a stump of old plum;

it used to bloom here
ripe with the scent

of expectations hung on it
over the years.

When we leave no one will know
that it stood there

between clothesline and fence
where our lives twisted and bellied out

in the wind.
I used to stand at that window

loving the scotch pines,
loving the shirts on the line

and the blue flags of my cotton skirts.
We'd blossom like that forever

I thought
leaving a print on the air.

Epithalamium: Pebbles

One on another
letting the stream have them

without knowing the plan.
Look at their long travail

out of the flow,
how they faced

the apocalypse, air,
cookies in God's pan

stalled in what must have been
at least a familiar pleasure.

One diva of a volcano
threw them up here

part of a cooled shelf
over the inland sea

etched here and there by mollusks,
shamans, small boys.

Broken and broken again,
they learned to take it

without bitching,
rolling around on each other

till smooth,
learning to get along.

Advance Warning

Look out, the village
is spilling its wraiths.

They slide over the river,
its bland face refusing to know.

The dogs' hairs stand on their spines,
feeling the passage of chilly animals

who do not offer the lifted tail
not eager to touch noses

not sharing the bowl.

Weather

I wake to the sound of rivers
rushing somewhere

perhaps out of my dream.
God sent the waters

above and below
like dogs

to their separate corners—
but people who live near rivers

keep looking for leaks.
I go downstairs in bare feet

to check the foundation.
My neighborhood holds:

Harry is drying the sparkplugs
ready to drive Helen to chemo.

Kate phones me to take the kids
to the crisis nursery.

It has rained for three weeks.

Hospice

I'm learning to wear grief
like an old coat. Too hot
for the season. No place
to lay it down.

I paint my house red.
I think of old barns in the snow
anointed with milk and blood.
Waste nothing: cover yourself

in the gore of the work. Even God
lived with the dead. I want to burn
something into the white hill of my life.
We are that used to wanting

we can't think of shedding a good coat
leaving it there for the mice
to take home in bits
each fiber bound for a nest.

You tell me this weather wastes
nothing, uncovers the heart's bone.

I Dream about Houses

I dream about houses
we used to live in, closed forever
to my kind, the locks changed

through which my ghost
easily streams, critiquing
the new décor

the andirons, the fake
colonial pewter. I take
from their drawers

rubber bands, potato peelers,
incriminating correspondence,
sex toys. One day I stole

their goldfish. Sometimes
I bend over the bed
not malevolent but unwilling

to lend them a breath from my store
of terrors behind that wall-
paper. Sometimes I pull

the coverlet over a cold foot,
draw the blinds. They'll need
to make friends with me

if they want me to be alarm
clock or therapist. There are things
I could tell them about the furnace.

They have only to ask.

Wash

She can check the neighboring lines
from her second-floor window

though the brides hang their underwear
in the middle, as mothers taught—

it's nobody's business you have
your monthlies.

The daring peignoirs of the next garden:
no overalls, or work pants

stretched on metal contraptions
that look like the outlines of men

who jumped out of the frame.
She thinks of the neighbor's space

between silk panty and garter
when Will comes home for lunch

from the Great Northern Yards,
crumbles saltines in his soup.

She can name every breeze that visits
the body behind that fence.

Becoming Conscious

Once I was the pool
owning today a sky
tonight a moon

    cloud
    heron
    star.

Over eons I learned
water:
a bowl in the rock
liking it well

    to fill
    empty
    and fill.

Education

Children should be seen and not heard.
Children should stand on a cliff
ready to whir

into the blackberry vines and needles
of rough juniper.
Children should not scream as they fall,

children should remain visible at all
times, quiet as clouds, while falling.
Only the mother's shout may be heard,

she also falling, calling out
whatever a mother voices,
permitted at last to cry.

Role Models: *Little Women*

Marmee had headaches, Father was gone.
Hannah scrubbed and got up before dawn.
Meg had a dutiful husband and bent her head
to the household yoke. Jo played hockey
and wanted to smoke thin brown cigars
with the publishing interns in some other book.
Did anyone want to be Amy? I think not.
Silly poodle, deserved what she got:
a rich husband with eyes for Jo.
Beth's talent turned out to be dying,
instead of piano, passing out bones
of love to each pilgrim until she was done.
We could be patient as she was,
she didn't live long.

Reunion Photos

The dead girl's hairstyle
will never change.

Without aging, she'll grow
unfashionable

without waking
be stylish again

look fresh in the center part
with her ironed planes

retro and ready to go.
Always something of high school

embarrassed
about her smile

as if she wants to ask you
for something you can't give.

High School: *Memento Mori*

All the girls in Commercial
are virgins, except Rita

they sent to the Good Shepherd Home.
I cannot tell you

the name of the easiest tree,
or the first declension. In Typing

we tap out our lines with a bell
at each stop. Miss Irmegard

Brookner teaches home ec. No girl
in Commercial is cute as the girls in

Prep. Outside hangs the world,
that green thing. I come

into homeroom at half past.
Carmen whispers my legs

have red welts from his vinyl
car seats. Miss Brookner's stockings

have thick, black seams.

Anorexia

She was full for a while
then he cheated on her
as she put it.

I think of Girl Scout card games,
evasions at odds-and-eves.
Having no word but the body

she starves again,
making a billboard
out of her skin

on which he can read the story
of how she is nothing to him.

Sleeping with Atheists

The Mennonite girls at the bus stop
shake boys from their skirts.
Prayer caps pinned to coiled hair
glow with bluing and starch.

When the nuns look away,
the Catholic girls turn a tuck
at their plaid waists. Thighs
welcome the sun's hand.

There is no bus they can get on
that won't drive them to town.

Men who do not believe
in God will try them, pretend
the sounds they make
are not prayers. Even the nuns
will have shut the high windows,
descended the stairs.

Learning America on the *Empire Builder*

1.

Just west of Williston, sky's the actor.
Buttes: prehistoric shrug of animals
letting it go, silt sifting down till
farm after farm climbed them and broke in its turn.

Nothing can live here: his voice in the dining car.

The border. My father's assessing glance
values each gold wire of my braids.
Twenty horn buttons fasten a wool coat,
behind each button a coin.
No jewels in my ears; they are sewn
into the pintucks of each sleeve.

Geese fly out of the slough. He regrets
the waste of space in those bodies
air sacs unoccupied; as they ascend,
their free flight.
       In the old photo, my sister's
querulous baby gaze. Holding her hand I felt
each pearl in her mitten fingers. Loud girls
on the playground talk softball, not watching
their things: what luxury. I look for hinges wherever.
Arithmetic books deliver the codes of Swiss banks.
Running for base, toes flinch from gold rings
under the pads of my shoes.

2.

A junkyard full of old woodies, wrecked
school buses, double-wides. I want to stop here,
live in a burnt car. Spend each year a button.
Pheasants get up from their corn, flaunt tails
they've earned. The *Empire Builder* burns
its long face into the smoke of the high plains.

Rain opens the next act. Cattle clump
under thunderheads, heifers walk in a line
resolute, as though one has a grip
on what might be fitting to do. The train
wails its doppler. After a while
rusty cars driven or dragged their last
cough's length to the end of the field
become lovely. Holiness enters again
turquoise fins and the Cessna's carapace
lifts on its wind.

3.

On the roof of the Tip-It Bar in Havre, Montana,
Santa—in March—still on the roof. Maybe
that's where he ran out of luck. Last child
of this world growing old. Blizzards begin
out of Cutback, gulleys and sloughs white.
Sudden as mountains things change. In 1887
avalanche closed the tracks. Travelers
picnicked. Bored youngsters descended the slope.

Curtains of snow slid over the lives of others. *Here*
is their willow cross. Rounding the bend ahead
the engine, blind as a worm, makes it,
heads into miles of tunnel. Red lights blink
go. We emerge into black spruce, granite,
streams frozen in midair over the gorge.

My life was that way a long time: now it runs free.
When the engineer enters a tunnel, still does his doubt
begin? How long can he ride through the dark
without screaming? Has he begun to know?

Where the slope is sleek and perfect
there you get slides.

Saturdays in America

December 8, 1956. Maria Callas sings *Lucia* at the Met.
The year we came to America, here to this kitchen.

My mother sits down on the linoleum
where she starts crying, housedress

rutched over her knees. She whimpers
about the voice *that it should be on the radio*

that we should have a radio. Pity the tenor
who has to finish that act. Concentration and hush

of anyone's mad scene. My father closes the book,
takes off his wire-rims, goes to her there on the tiles,

smoothing, smoothing her stockings. Between acts,
the perfect English of Milton Cross

gives him verb after verb to carry her home
without falling out of America. *That he could*

rock her like that, their hands undoing each other
while I sit, eating baloney with ketchup on Wonder

Bread, here in America. He croons her back across ice
where the coloratura also skates for e over high c.

They come down into the body, disheveling as they leave
me to my lunch, glass breaking all over the kitchen.

And she keeps singing, she sings.

The Apartment

The stone sink was deep and flared at one end
into lines like those a river leaves on sand
where you'd stand things to dry: the daily china,
its blue rim, flowers I'd say, but I can't see them
now; the mind takes things into its pockets

yet I remember green furze on the ottoman
how the clock whirred before hours as if it gathered
itself to be truthful. Streetcars rattled, saying no lovers
ever got on, it's all cells, crypts, and hospitals
at the end of the line. We weren't unhappy, just

it had come down to this: visits from clean old
priests, their pink knotted clutch on the chair arms
my dress itchy, my toys put away, wondering
why does he sit there forever, why does he stay?

Photo: Father, Daughter, 1932

The man who died young
wears blue, matching
the hand-colored sky.
Some photo-assistant had her way

with the dapper apparel,
reddened the girl's lips.
The bull terrier, Mike,
strains at his leash

starts forward
as if he alone
can foresee the consequences.
The back of his head

reflects in the car's mirror.
He has gravity.
Only the dog
has a hold on life.

Clearing Out the Dead

People leave their bodies
more easily than their clothes.
His shoulder bones rattle around
in a sheepskin jacket
hung on the porch.

Yet when I saw him *laid*
as they say *out*
he had without question
departed that bag of tricks.

We give up our lives,
hang on to the things
we shopped for.
I tried to wear myself
into her pink robe,
she pushed from inside
till I gave it away.

They fold themselves
in the wardrobe
breathing
what's left of the air.

Doctors

Doctors made house calls then
mostly, you say, on the wives
who hadn't wanted the child at first
who think their ambivalent care
filled its throat with a spider
confection of thrush.

You finish the chapter for her
drinking coffee there by the sink.
You don't sit down. In the mirror
of the toaster you see her life
read it all
like a symptom.

A Memorial Image of the Angel of Death

Incongruous clothing, embroidery,
etching on buckle. It gets in the way

of the flight, yet she must have it.
Majolica makes us look silly,

fat blooming twin under each arm,
though they were hydrocephalic.

The sculptor takes up my burden
of crazy mercy. Love is all daft.

She must mourn a tangible form
to stand in for what she has lost,

simply a vision at this point:
how things should have been.

Yet the night is thick with our wings
and the fuss we make over these infants,

air never their element, earth their ground.

Cassandra at the Train

I linger between cars on the station platform:
wait, a girl out of Edward Hopper,
pale face under the arc light.

You clatter past, warm bowl of the pipe
in your hand, sanguine and comfortable.
You can't stop. Not even the cord

strung for emergencies works.
Panic and scream at the engineer
as you will, you are lost now

for—that English word—*ever.*
I cried it out long ago, stand
arms crossed, holding the strap

of a shoulder bag. You reach for me
always, hurtling through the dark.

Sellers Motivated

For a while the house
sagged on itself
then new people
moved in
with teacups that chink
in a different key
from the teacups
that lived there before.

An innocent
pouring of coffee,
a holding themselves apart.
A surreptitious glance
into my garden
as though I grew
rare greens. How hard
will they struggle
to heal that house?
Or will the cat
they took in
rend the curtains
and rain pour over
the sills at last?

Ghosts

That buzz at the kitchen window:
moths to the living
who are like light to them,
tomatoes ripe on the sill
veins of the man's arm as he lifts
the newspaper.

They are greedy for each day
held in the cells of fruit—
maybe the whole summer:
how she bends over the vines
trims off blighted leaves
her expectation for all it will be.

Even the dog on the floor
imagining drama,
in which his nobility, wisdom
and kindness surpass the president's
on the radio calming the population
in time of war—
the ghosts covet.

How full the living are
and how sated, the ghosts say
hearing him call her over and over
out of the place
she'd get lost in otherwise.

Every detail of this picture
the dead know, *taken in,*
they flail at the boundary
keeping them out in the cold,
becoming an agitation
there at the edge of the curtains
becoming bold.

War Dogs

Reporting from Baghdad, Haifa, Beirut,
the announcer's voice breaks up in static
and gunnery rattle—*there,* hear it?—
the steady bark of some medium dog
the generic desert breed, liminal dog
who stands on the rubble
outside the Grand Hotel.

The BBC girl-under-fire fades in and out
but the bark's pulse researching its mayday
goes on. A chipmunk stands in my yard,
takes in the berserk barking off NPR.
Bees on sunflowers tap their feet.
Everything runs. Star, Shep, and Queenie,
even Pookie and Muffin yap.

Gifted

People who listen
hear so much
they can't stand it.

They have to go to the woods
or the top of some mountain
maybe the Mall of America

some place the ambient noise
keeps down screaming; soon
they receive the gift

of the language of rabbits, cicadas,
shopgirls, shoplifters,
immigrant women who clean toilets

and keep the elevator charging
from floor to floor. There is no place
they can't hear the cries.

One of them lives under a bridge
with his dog, a master of inattention,
bestowing the cold lick;

away from home mostly
unable to answer the phone.

Reaching the Basement

Coming to scrub the fourth corner,
chip loose paint off cement
stuck with old stones,

I wonder who wrote in pencil *here!*
yummy!—and why? Yesterday,
pushing a broom into the struts

under the stairs, I clinked
on a bottle of bath salts
labeled in deco style.

Thirty years in this house.
I've touched the penultimate pebble,
flushed out the spiders,

the buffalo nickel, the boyfriend's
dime bag over the workbench,
hairpins galore. The old yellow

and blue layers, loved like frescoes,
shine in scrub water, sauna smell
of pine shelving, a slick place where aprons

polish the wall when we turn,
laundry basket on hip. Down-cellar the dead
are thickest, so much wash to do

and during the work, so much
to think over. Lines of housedresses,
white shirts and underwear wrung

and pegged to the winter lines.
I think we return
to what we were thinking about

sooner than anything done. We were so
interruptible: maybe it's only the basement
we managed to fill.

Calling Them Home

She polished the woodwork
put away knick-knacks

hung a mirror
at the top of the stair

set out a plate and cup. Now
she cuts from its wrinkled

skin a ripe mango; the bread
its scent live and salt

in the room.
Something may enter

inhabit the clear space
turn to its home.

Women's Prayers

In the mountains
where God walks
they lift like smoke,
each particle clear
to the God-eye.

Mary, Jane, Chang-Mee
Yvette, even the girls
with numbers or days
of the week for names,
he knows them.

He walks
through the cloud of them
wearing their cries
for a cloak.

He hums a little,
comforting them,
calling to girls
like a bee.

Whenever he comes out
prayers settle,
a fur on his shoulders,
trying to get an ear.

He keeps himself
in a kind of trance
not letting one or another
get close. At night

he dreams of their
willfully quilting him;
when he turns over
they tickle his loins.

The Fisherman's Wife

That is his hair, red sea wrack
gold tipped. Those are the bloodless

roots of his fingers, teeth among
cowrie shells shot here and there

tongue of an eel
bottom feeder

moving on viscous suckers
over the weir.

One day, maybe,
I would have cut him

into this many bits
had not his last cast

in a windstorm
taken my part

as the wind sometimes does
being herself homeless

wailing to get in or out.
There are his walleyes

that is the bait of his snout
The long-whiskered bludgeons

of trash fish pick up
without prejudice

women's prayers.

Watching the End of the World from Hovland, Minnesota

RAVENS

It's north enough here for ravens:
that raucous note
that blade through dinner
delivers its say
the story we never listened to
sounding like *go*
or *stay*. Does it matter?

Raven's contempt
for the weak is a matter of record.
Odin, old One-Eye
at the door covets a sandwich.
Under our grace, the food cools.
You uncap the home-beer,
we live together as if patience
could hold off the wind.

THE LETTER

Shadow out of the west
like a line of whales
behind it a quilt of light.
Gulls endure without fishing
cycles of night and day
preferring neither,
till one rides up, delivers
the day's letter from that creation
its holy way.

Breath slows to wave action
on fundament. Here we can call
and answer each other
with pure sound.

SWIMMING THE TEMPERANCE GORGE

Under Temperance Falls, dense water
feels like froth when you surface,
kill fast. You choke if you're lucky
and look surprised.

The spirit, at death,
lifts through a hinge in the skull:
birdprints of creation a newborn
keeps open for options.
The body is not a closed system.
We are veiling adrift, sea jelly.

A German exchange student hunting
for verbs, climbs out of the river.
You carry the dogs over currents
they won't swim.

Each day
we close the hatch of the fontanel
cease communication with outside
make a decision to stay. Each year
we dive to more dangerous caves
look for new hand-holds,
making our bodies small.

BATS

Couriers between worlds
climb over the sill;
pleats of their thorned
wings rattle with tales
shed in the slither and haste,
carried so far. I wake
to their mild imperative
keening. Out of the west
a surf rises. Rain.
You croon in your love
promise sorrow from which
you cannot protect me.
Lovers are that psychic.

Beyond our pocket of woods
maybe the world has exploded.
We will find out one day
how the thing ended.

Morels on goat prairie gloat
in their blue light. Spruce
speaking of green on green.

Naming Dogs

Star! I call her. Who knows
what may answer?
Beware what you yell out the door.

Don't name your dog Bowser
or syllables in Chinese
that mean *death*.

I'll give you Bowser
something is waiting to answer,
ready to spring.

All down the street
people are tempting fate
calling for Angel and Boots.

Who whistled the dog
of the current administration?
Star! I call. *Beauty!* and *Goodness!*

Each dog feathers his prayer flag
of a tail in the public square
comes at a run.

www.ingramcontent.com/pod-product-compliance
Lightning Source LLC
Chambersburg PA
CBHW021346090426
42742CB00008B/762